Live Rich n Die Rich

K Firose Khan

Copyright © 2023 by K Firose Khan

All rights reserved.

This book or any portion thereof may not be reproduced or used in any manner whatsoever without the express written permission of the respective writer of the respective content except for the use of brief quotations in a book review.

The writer of the respective work holds sole responsibility for the originality of the content and The Write Order is not responsible in any way whatsoever.

Printed in India

ISBN: 978-93-5776-970-9

First Printing, 2023

The Write Order
A division of Nasadiya Technologies Private Ltd.
Koramangala, Bengaluru
Karnataka-560029

THE WRITE ORDER PUBLICATIONS.

www.thewriteorder.com

Edited by Literary Connect

Typeset by MAP Systems, Bengaluru

Book Cover designed by Sankhasubhro Nath

Publishing Consultant - Priyanka Lal

I did not start out rich. There were times when I did not have enough food or even ten rupees to fill the petrol tank of my Kawasaki Bajaj motorcycle. I still have it as a memento of my hard times. In my late 20s and early 30s, I never had any extra money to kick-start a fortune. It seemed like there were always insufficient resources to pay my bills, and every rupee I earned was absorbed. I was consistently in debt.

The idea of becoming rich was a distant dream with almost no possibility of coming true. But there was a shift when I decided to start with desire. If I sincerely wanted to leave the odds behind, achieve financial independence, and retire rich, there were four crucial steps I took, all starting with the letter 'D.' The first step is desire. You must want it, make an unshakeable commitment, and be ready to make sacrifices. The second 'D' is a decision. I needed to make a decision right now to do whatever was necessary, to be willing to pay any price, and to go any distance to achieve my goal. The third 'D' is determination—to keep at it until I succeed despite all the problems and obstacles I might encounter. The fourth 'D' is discipline—the discipline to master and develop the habits necessary for achieving financial independence. Those are the four Ds: desire, decision, determination, and discipline. You can measure how successful you will be in the future by measuring how well you're doing in each of these D's on a scale of one to ten.

First, you have to make a beginning and make a decision right now that you are going to achieve financial independence, no matter what obstacles you face in the short term. It makes a significant difference when you write it down, create a plan, and start working on it every single day.

Second, have the resolve in advance that you will persist even when you face setbacks. You will never give up. You will continue to move forward until you finally achieve your goal.

I have been following these fundamental principles, and they have never failed me. I must acknowledge the gratitude I felt for so many people in my initial years of struggle. I dedicate this book to the network business, without which I wouldn't be what I am today. I express my gratitude to this brilliant form of business that has helped me make my fortune. You can do the same if you follow the principles outlined in this book. My heartfelt gratitude to my mentors and friends who trusted me when nobody in the world was ready to do so and had unflinching faith in me!

Foreword

Today, wealth has become a measure of the value we add to our lives. It is impossible to have a decent life without money, yet very few have mastered it. Not many have mastered the art of creating abundance. How about learning to invite abundant money into your life, ensuring that it never recedes, and making sure it keeps growing with every passing day? In this book, we explore the freedom that money awards to an achiever and what financial freedom denotes. We will also examine what is stopping you from achieving this much-needed financial freedom. Make currency work for you, even if you don't!

I always wanted to live a life of abundance, and who wouldn't? We want to enjoy our youth with more than sufficient purchasing power and enter old age with complete financial security, knowing that our years were full of rich experiences and that we spent them doing something that mattered.

Throughout our lives, we make decisions to maximize our happiness or fulfill our desires. Money is the medium to get what we want; it allows us to buy the things we desire, trade our time for money through jobs, and use that money to acquire more of what we want. This cycle continues.

Life has many aspects that make it fulfilling. A happy family life and good health are among the other important aspects of life. Now, we must decide whether having more money is more important than having more of these other aspects. Should you devote a large percentage of your time to maximizing money at the expense of other areas? In the book, I explain the three Fs, or F3, and how to strike a balance among all three factors.

The idea behind writing this book is to remove the idea of 'Lack' from our lives. Money is often blamed for many problems in life. Poor people wish they were richer; some not-so-poor people wish they were richer so they could travel the world; and poor students wish they had more money to get a better education. The idea is to propel one's life from better to better, wanting to graduate from getting paid for what they love to getting paid extremely well for doing what they are extremely passionate about.

I also emphasize that to achieve abundance, we have to be passionate about what we do, whether in entrepreneurship or employment. We can't merely 'like' the activities we are involved in; to plan an abundant future in every way, we have to love them with all our hearts and complete passion, helping them earn millions for us. Unless we give 100 percent to what we are involved in, we cannot expect excellent returns. We must immerse our hearts and souls in it, not only to achieve prosperity but in significant quantities. In doing so, we should ensure that we neither obsess over money nor neglect other avenues of a quality life, such as our family and health. Still, the intensity and passion to earn massive amounts of money must constantly burn within us.

The Wonder Of The F3

The three F's are finance, family, and fitness. These three aspects are the cornerstones of life, and organizing them will provide the foundation for success in the areas you choose.

Financial Fitness: It's obvious that financial status is an essential contributor to our happiness. When we earn handsomely and handle money wisely, giving it an appropriate amount of significance in our lives—not too little, not too much—it makes us happy and greatly contributes to our fulfillment and contentment. The Consumer Financial Protection Bureau (CFPB) defines financial well-being as: "Financial well-being can be defined as a state of being wherein a person can fully meet current and ongoing financial obligations, can feel secure in their financial future, and can make choices that allow enjoyment of life."

For our well-being, we need to have enough money to establish a plush lifestyle and maintain it comfortably. It allows one to make choices that allow enjoyment of life, such as having a good house to live in, having plenty of money to start a family and keep it in a happy zone, and keeping oneself fit and healthy. All these aspects of life require a fat wallet. Thus, we should have enough money to buy products and experiences that we enjoy using now and in the future.

You can start steering your financial situation in the right direction by:

1. Learning how to stack the financial odds in your favor.

2. Developing savings for retirement, the children's college, or maybe for the next financial emergency.

3. Keep your financial house in order—and keep it that way.

Not just a better life, but the best life is a possibility, as you do have the power to change things for the better. "From Now to Financial Happiness" is your roadmap to financial freedom. When you achieve financial freedom, your life suddenly changes from destiny-driven to self-driven, and the surprising effect of this is that you are suddenly stripped of all excuses for why your life might be less than ideal. Thus, you become solely responsible for your happiness, not allowing any excuses.

The lesson should be that considering financial well-being only in terms of how much we can buy or consume presents an incomplete and perhaps even misleading picture about the role that money plays in our lives. Our relationship with money need not be centered on constantly buying new things and feeling less stressed and more secure when we can do so. Financial well-being needs a third dimension that measures the joy and contentment that come from leading a full life in which money plays a remarkably supportive role instead of being the showstopper.

Family being the very basis of society, time spent with it becomes the key to one's happiness. Quality family time together is the ultimate luxury, and almost all agree that family is central to our identity and happiness. Family plays a significant role when it is functioning properly and is a place of refuge and restoration. It provides a place where we can establish meaningful relationships. The pressures and stressors of the world can sometimes feel like scraped skin, and to counteract this, we build a family where we can love and be loved. Family is the place where you can be encouraged, affirmed, and have fun. Yes, indeed, happiness is strongly tied to changes in the quality of family relationships and, over time, much less strongly tied to changes in income. The well-being of the family can be attained by observing how people allocate their time; you are bound to get a different idea. A balance between a relentless pursuit of materialism and wholesome family pursuits is the key to happiness. It has been seen very often that, in the absence of enough money, love doesn't last very long. The struggles of life start taking a toll on the finer nuances of love. You cannot survive just spending quality time with your spouse and children; you also need to earn extremely well to maintain a good flow of income to handle day-to-day living expenses. Family means a setting for personal growth where you get a warm feeling of security, to have someone who you can count on, whom you can share your problems with, but it also means to be responsible: to fend for their lives of comfort.

Fitness: Health is the bedrock for attaining every other valuable resource in life. Without health, do you have the capacity to create wealth or raise a family? With a chronic lack of access to the means for healthy living, it becomes harder to build up a wealth of life experiences. When our energy is consistently consumed by efforts to achieve or maintain a basic level of health, there's little left over to devote to achieving anything else. The more time you spend on survival, the less time you have left to focus on thriving.

A fit person can enjoy what life has to offer, create experiences, and cherish all that money can buy. Money can buy most things in life, but it can't buy health. However, when you are ill, you need money to get medical treatment from doctors. You have to be well-endowed to buy treatments, and then there would be an enhancement in the quality of life, as you would have regained the ability to experience joy and share it with others. Yes, the best way to be a truly wealthy person is to protect the health of your body, mind, and spirit and have enough bank balance to get the best treatment in the world as and when necessary.

Health needs to be understood holistically to understand how everything else flows from it. A healthy body comprises the state of your body, mind, and spirit as an integrated whole. And this integrated whole directly impacts your experience of wealth. Suppose you are a rich person who is physically healthy but has toxic thoughts about others. Eventually, your wealth will never be enough, and it will never satisfy you because your ability to experience gratitude and delight will be compromised. In comparison with a person who respects his body, feeds his mind, and nurtures his spirit by showing compassion to others, he will enjoy his wealth as a blessing—and most likely, it will be shared, thus perpetuating the cycle of good health and goodwill. It is also true that when you have a reasonable amount of wealth stacked away, you feel more secure and confident in life, thus improving its well-being. A cocktail of good health, high spirits, and a stable and happy mind with a fat bank balance isn't a bad deal at all. It is not necessary that a wealthy person have a toxic mindset.

Nowadays, people have become conscious, and awareness has set in that, along with wealth, a healthy life of the body, mind, and spirit is essential and can go well hand-in-hand.

The F3 of finance, family, and fitness can be woven together and made into a beautiful tapestry of life.

Challenges Of A Goal

The challenge is to set a goal. Goal-setting can be very overwhelming. You start with great intentions to change things for the better, but by trying to do it on your own, without being accountable to anyone, and without any guidance, it can be extremely difficult to achieve. My challenge was that I was a couch potato, and my trials to get out of the rut were a Herculean task. The mistake that I kept repeating was that I just kept trying to apply it all in one go, and that wasn't working. I was going around in circles, doing a lot of planning to get started, leading to procrastination rather than just getting started instantly.

I cracked the code when I followed this principle in this phase of my life and later proved successful every time I used it. It is quite simple now; I know that I know the trick of just taking one part of your life and changing only that one thing. You build up that one thing in each area, and it works wonders. It could be just a small thing too, but it has a tremendous impact on your life, instantaneously.

Let me share a quick example. I looked at my life and knew I wanted to be healthier. Therefore, I decided to get up early in the morning and do a short walk at first, and when ready, turn that into a short jog. So I did. Three times a week, I'd get up earlier than usual and go for a short walk. The first few weeks were hard, as staying in bed always seemed like a better option, but I knew I needed to change. What I hadn't even considered were the other amazing benefits that came along.

Exercising on Monday, Wednesday, and Friday meant that my habit of having a few beers in the evening stopped, which had made it more difficult to get out of bed, saved money, and improved my health, etc.

Mornings became less stressful. Family breakfasts happened instead of rushing in the shower or having a shave.

I started going to bed earlier instead of sitting up late to watch TV on my own.

It was neither easy nor did it happen in one go. But I was soon able to apply this method to different areas of my life. I changed one thing each week and enjoyed feeling good about my transforming lifestyle. I feel that I have managed to balance my life. At times, there is a wobble, but it kind of settles down.

The biggest thing for me is that, as a family, we are closer than when I was a couch potato. I realized that there would always be several things I'd love to change, but they are out of my control. I am still a long way off perfect, but I am working on it, working on being the best version of myself.

The Trilogy Of T

Tired, Try, and Tomorrow are the terms that have to be deleted from our lives. Drop these negative words. Many times, we think that to solve a problem, we need to add something. The truth is, there are many situations when removing something is a more efficient solution. The words tired, try, and tomorrow fall into this category. These words act as a crutch we don't seem to get rid of.

Physical tiredness is a state of mind, and this feeling lies in the crevices of our mind. The mind is the decision-maker that declares that the body is fatigued, even before the muscles tire out. The brain gets the cue from the blood levels to send signals to the body that it is tired so that muscles are protected from exercising too hard.

It is mandatory that one can work for long hours by conditioning their mind against feeling tired, as this state of mind can be controlled effectively with regular practice. Suppose you have returned from a hard day's work and would like to crash into bed even with your shoes on, but you see your child, who is a toddler, trying to put his small hands into the burning stove. Would you continue to feel tired and stay still? NO. You would rush to save the child's hand and put off the stove. How could you do this when you were complaining of tiredness? You allow yourself the privilege to feel tired, so your body is tired. Deny it, and you will have no other option but to be full of energy.

A popular complaint is "I am tired all the time." Thankfully, it's not a medical issue; therefore, one can reverse it with a change of lifestyle. Tiredness can negatively impact performance at work, family life, and social relationships. The causes of tiredness could be reduced or no energy, physical or mental exhaustion, lack of motivation, staying up too late, having too much caffeine or alcohol, eating junk food, etc.

Staying organized, setting realistic goals, working on systems that help to remove stress and anxiety, worrying less (as it does not resolve problems but clogs clear thinking), taking frequent breaks, meditation, saying yes to self-acceptance, and caring for oneself are some of the antidotes to tiredness.

Regarding the notion of 'trying,' it can often be told whether certain people are going to be successful or if they're not going to be so by their language. Often, I have seen people come up to me all energized, but then I hear them make statements like, 'I'm going to try my best!'

When it comes to success in today's world, 'trying' simply is not good enough. You have to give whatever you are doing your best shot. Goals have to be realistic, of course. For example, I wouldn't be able to play on the Indian cricket team at the age of 40, however much I practice. But if I am instructed to submit a proposal to the HNI client on a certain date, I've got to do it. Just trying my best would fall short of the deadline, which could lead to losing the HNI client. That means a poor appraisal and, thus, a low increment. Trying is in contrast to the determination to complete the job within the specified period of time. It is important to have the fire in the belly burning on high, which would help in doing and achieving rather than just trying one's best. If you're on your journey to success and you find yourself saying that you're going to 'try,' then take a step back and make sure that you give your 200%. When you're all in, and if you suffer a setback, it is not forever! You are not a failure until you throw in the towel. Setbacks are going to happen in any endeavor you pursue. Their occurrence does not mean that you should quit. Lick your wounds, reassess the right course of action, and keep moving forward! Sometimes the effort alone may not be good enough. What was needed was the execution of the actual task or goal. That's the difference between winners and losers, in life and in general.

Tomorrow Never Comes!

Yesterday is history, tomorrow is a mystery, and only today is the gift in your hands, when you can do anything about anything.

"Tomorrow never comes" is a cardinal truth: no, tomorrow never comes, because when it does come, it's already today. When you wait for a particular tomorrow and are eager for it to arrive, the wait seems to take forever.

It is the nature of the human mind to postpone work until tomorrow. The mind has this habit of flitting from one thought to another. Now it depends on us how we seize the unstable mind, drag it from its wanderings, and fix it on one idea. This has to be done repeatedly, whenever it wanders away. However, most of us are unable to control our minds. We keep postponing the task at hand today to tomorrow, which never comes. As the great poet and spiritual leader Kabir says, "Tomorrow's work has to be done today, and today's work is now. If this moment is lost, the work will never get done." Once you indulge in procrastination, no one knows how 'tomorrow' will turn out to be or even whether we will be around or not. Time and tide wait for none. At the end of life's journey, all unfinished tasks will come to haunt us, and we will be full of remorse and regret. We have to train our minds to enjoy the present moment and conduct it in the way we know best to finish our work. We find a variety of excuses to not do the work at hand. This way, an entire life is wasted, and not much work gets done. As the deadline to finish a task gets closer, we get stressed and wonder what to do now. The habit of postponing work increases our stress levels. So it's better to do the day's work that very day and avoid postponing it to tomorrow.

It is necessary that you stop sabotaging yourself, figure out your patterns of behavior, and then find creative ways to counteract them and form new habits.

Strength Of The Mind

The time in which we live is turbulent. To overcome the turbulence, we need a strong and stable mind. Whatever the circumstances around us, we will need to rely on the mental toughness we normally look for in our heroes. We admire heroes about whom we have read in a book like Robin Hood and watched movies of James Bond because they embody the characteristics that we've valued throughout the ages. These heroes make us believe and feel what it's like to have the mental toughness to break out of our insignificant and boring worlds and step into a much bigger and more adventurous world, full of possibilities.

A strong mind has a great capacity to face challenges. Being strong means having the resources, mental skills, and physical capabilities to confront challenges of all kinds. A person with a strong mind has the energy and stamina to face challenges without being robbed of their inner strength. Mental toughness gives us the courage to outgrow the stress we experience in life. The secret ingredient of a strong mind is confidence, courage, commitment, control, and purpose. These characteristics can be harnessed, and a strong mind can be created to live larger than life. If these qualities are harnessed and displayed in your daily behavior, you become mentally tough, irrespective of what takes place in your life. These guiding principles will always give meaning to your life and take it to another level.

The five elements of a strong mind are not limited to the famed heroes but are for common people like you and me, with struggles and tough times, so that we can incorporate the good ones. Toughness in the spirit and soul can prove to be more useful than in the muscles. Building a strong mind is a lifelong task. It will not only pay off when obstacles are in your way, but it will also become a habit and eventually a part of your identity to be strong!

In life, you will come across situations that are easy and others that are hard, and the secret to thriving in any of these extreme contexts is to maintain an objective perspective. Mental strength allows you to see the situation as it is, which is essential to achieving success in such times. Stressful situations can weigh heavily on your heart and mind. If you allow them to do so, such circumstances can make you believe that things are much worse than they are. Being pessimistic about the situation can make you think that it is impossible to overcome; eventually, you lose heart and impair your ability to achieve peak performance.

When you have a strong mind, it helps you not to despair during hard times. Through mental strength, you can identify the problem spots and magnify the situation. Developing the ability to gain insight into tough situations can help keep an even keel and achieve success. Being mentally strong, you can learn how to overcome the discomfort that impedes you from achieving your goals, set realistic targets, and meet them even in the face of opposing emotions and thoughts.

Fight To Live Rich And Die Rich

For most people, wealth doesn't simply come one day. Getting rich takes sustained work and backbreaking effort. Just as a person desiring to lose weight has to be disciplined enough to get up early every day without fail and exercise, Similarly, to become rich, you have to give up your comforts and literally step out of your comfort zone. You have to get used to being uncomfortable. Becoming a wealthy person isn't easy, and the need for comfort can be devastating. It is best to learn to be comfortable while operating in a state of ongoing uncertainty.

It has been seen that, generally, the rich are typically self-employed, while average people tend to settle for steadier situations. You've got to ditch the steady paycheck. That's not to say you should quit your day job right now. Instead, start something on the side, says Daymond John, a self-made millionaire who lived on the tips he received waiting tables at Red Lobster while launching the clothing line that would evolve into billions of dollars.

Too many people let their fear hold them back from making important decisions. But someday you're going to fail at something. Let that not bother you. Instead of being afraid to take risks, each opportunity has to be seen as a way to learn new skills. As Richard Branson says, "nobody gets everything right the first time. Business is like a giant game of chess—you have to learn quickly from your mistakes. Successful entrepreneurs don't fear failure; they learn from it and move on."

Jim Rohn states that the greatest reward in becoming a millionaire is the kind of person that you have to become to become a millionaire, not the amount of money that you earn.

Most people wish their circumstances would magically change for them and don't kindle the desire to become better so they can proactively improve their own circumstances. By simply waiting and wishing for luck, you can seek to become the kind of person equipped with the skills to do brilliant things. Therefore, the quality of who you are as a person and the work you do is completely within your control, and you must become the kind of person who naturally attracts the success you seek. It's only when you invest in something that you have the motivation to make it happen. Your number one investment must be yourself.

The focus of the richest people is on earning, and typically, they aren't content with one source of revenue. Instead of relying on one singular source of income, find out several avenues for income generation. Wealthy, successful people are also very particular about who they associate with. Their goal is to develop relationships with other success-minded individuals because you become like the people you associate with, and that's why winners are attracted to winners.

When left to their own devices, most people waste their time. Only by investing your time well can you get a good return on that time. You have to realize that nearly every second spent on social media is wasted time. You can't have that time back. Rather than making your future better, it actually makes your future worse. Garbage in is garbage out. On the other hand, every invested moment leaves you better off. The world's most successful people are intense learners, mainly hard readers. They know that what they know determines how well they see the world. They know that what they know determines the quality of the relationships they can have and the quality of work they can do.

If you are to become rich, you must work to learn. Unsuccessful people work primarily for money. It is by "sharpening your saw" that you'll continue to become a better and more capable person. Thus, as you dedicate large portions of time to becoming a better thinker and communicator and more skilled in your craft, the quality of your work will continue to increase. Eventually, you'll be able to charge high fees for your work because no one else can do it like you. You will find yourself less distracted than most people are when they work. While working, you can get more done in a few hours because your time is spent well. Your priorities are clear, you're well rested, and your mind is stimulated. When you learn something, you should get a return on that learning. If you do not learn, you are wasting your time.

Even those who have high incomes are not truly wealthy because their lifestyles are such that they make more and consume more. Very few people make enough money to invest that money. It's best to think of your business as only half of your income equation. You have your business, which brings in income. Then, you have your investment entity to turn your income into more money. Investing money is how you will get super-rich since the reason to save money is to one day invest it. Their wealth isn't measured by the amount they make each year, but by how they've saved and invested over time.

The rich spend some time, say 20 minutes, to devote themselves to learning a new skill. Wealthy people are dedicated to self-improvement. Get out of your comfort zone, engage in a new activity that causes discomfort, and grow as an individual. It could be reading a book about an unfamiliar topic, taking a class or joining a local networking group, or going on a trek.

The most important thing is to start today. Tomorrow is uncertain.

Getting rich is quite different from staying rich. To get rich, you can start a business, save and invest wisely, inherit money, get lucky, etc. But staying rich is quite a challenge since you again have to work on your self-awareness, modesty, and the ability to delay gratification with a portion of your capital. Take care, as money can corrupt even the best of intentions, and it's significant that no matter how much you make, you still have to save to build actual wealth.

Life

Yes, life is beautiful, but it doesn't stop there. Life is not always easy. Life brings problems now and then, and the challenge lies in facing them with courage and dignity. Only when we deal with these challenges does the beauty of life reveal itself and act as a balm, making the ordeal bearable. Hope seeps in during these trying times. Joy, sorrow, victory, defeat, good moments, and bad moments are different sides of the same coin. All of us, however powerful, wise, or rich, have experienced suffering and failure. Life is beautiful, and every moment should be a celebration of being alive, since you never know when your time is up and, swoosh, you are gone. In spite of its unpredictable nature, one should always be ready to face adversity and challenges. Only when a person encounters difficulties in life can they achieve success.

It is during difficult times that you undergo tests for courage, patience, perseverance, and your true character. It is this adversity and hardship that make a person strong and ready to face the challenges of life with equanimity. Without pain, nothing can be gained. Success is nourished and sustained only when one toils and sweats for it.

Thus, life is not a bed of roses; it comes with thorns and should be accepted by us just as we accept the beautiful side of life. Everything is transitory, and so are the roses and the thorns.

The thorns serve as a reminder that both success and happiness are elusive, and thus we need not feel disappointed and disheartened. But we should remember that the pain of thorns is short-lived, and the beauty of life will soon overcome the prick of thorns. The disillusionment that any situation would persist for long might cause depression and frustration. One who faces difficulties and accepts success with equanimity is the one who will experience real happiness, contentment, and peace in life.

Love

All of us have an intense desire to be loved and nurtured, which is considered one of our most basic needs. One of the forms in which this need manifests is contact comfort—the desire to be held and touched. For example, babies who are deprived of contact comfort, particularly during the first six months after they are born, grow up to be psychologically damaged. A crucial factor determining our happiness is whether we feel sufficiently loved and cared for. Having healthy relationships leads to a happy and fulfilling life. Similarly, there is a desire to love and take care of others.

There is a deep-seated desire to love and care for others, and since this is quite hard-wired, the fulfillment of this desire enhances our happiness levels. The expression of love or compassion for others benefits both the recipient of affection and the person who delivers it. It has been observed that even small acts of kindness generate just as much happiness as lofty acts.

We are happy if we are the recipients of others' attention, love, and respect, rather than the donors of attention, love, and respect. Happiness does not lie in achieving self-enhancing goals such as career success, wealth, fame, or power. It is the need to love and care for others that should be emphasized.

Love is much more than simply choosing to spend your life with someone. It is like waking up every morning and choosing to spend the rest of your life with them. Love is not passive but a perpetual action of choice.

When you love somebody or something, you do so with complete dedication and involvement because this is a journey that cannot be partially traveled. You are in it completely. Love is as critical as oxygen is for your mind and body. It's not negotiable. If you are more connected, you will be healthier, both physically and emotionally. The less connected you are, the more you are at risk—the risk of exposure to illnesses, both physical and mental. The less love you have in your life, the more depression you are likely to experience. It has been seen that depressed people neither love themselves nor feel loved by others.

The important notion is that love is an action actively put into action, not passive acceptance. To give is defined as a great manifestation of love when a person can give without demanding something in return. It is obvious that it doesn't matter how a person understands love; it only matters how he or she feels it. Love in marriage, family, romantic relationships, or any other form influences a person's life and can become the sense of his or her life.

Happiness

"I have all that I need in life—money, property, relationships, comforts, and even luxury. What's wrong if I have just that? What is that extra bit that I get from being happy? Does being happy matter?

Happiness doesn't just feel good; happy people are more successful in many areas of life, like marriage, friendship, income, work, charity, and health. Happier people earn more. People who are happier with their lives have been found to have higher incomes and more material wealth. The United Nations World Happiness Survey, published in 2015, found that throughout the world, income is the primary predictor of happiness, and the more you make, the happier you become. Similarly, being happy makes us successful, rather than success making us happy.

Happy people are more likely to excel in job interviews and secure better jobs. They are evaluated more positively by superiors at work, exhibit higher performance and productivity, and handle managerial positions better. Happiness also enhances your productivity and problem-solving abilities. In a job, a happy person is more likely to succeed. They exhibit less disruptive behavior and are less prone to burnout due to work.

Happy people are more 'pro-social' and inclined to help others. They are more likely to volunteer compared to their unhappy counterparts. Happy people have more friends, better social support, and are more satisfied with their friends and group activities. They experience less jealousy, maintain stronger family connections, have more fulfilling marriages, and tend to be more satisfied with their marriages, leading to better physical and mental health.

Contrary to the belief that healthy people are happier, it is often seen that people spend the best years of their lives trying to make money but sacrifice their health and family. Eventually, they spend the rest of their days using that same money to recover their lost health and estranged relationships. A person is truly happy when they can make the most of favorable times and cope effectively with inevitable challenges, leading to the best possible overall life experience.

Happiness is what we desire most, not only for ourselves but also for our loved ones. We want our loved ones to be happy, often at the cost of our own happiness. That's why it matters so much.

Zach Holz's happiness quadrant provides a systematic way to evaluate choices and actions to optimize happiness. The four aspects are money, community, purpose, and health. The more these aspects positively impact our lives, the happier we feel. Having less money can lead to debt and stress. If you struggle to pay credit card bills and mortgages, you might feel compelled to keep a job even if you dislike it, which can lead to prolonged exposure to stress and resulting health issues. Having money provides us with options for more enjoyable alternatives and allows us to spend more time with family and friends. Joy in our lives comes from the communities we support and those that support us. Our deep connection with these identities determines our happiness. Having a sense of purpose when we wake up in the mornings helps us approach activities with a happy frame of mind. Often, a person's job provides them with a sense of purpose and happiness. Health is the fourth part of the quadrant and is a strong determinant of our happiness. Chronic illness can diminish our zest for life. We need to identify which aspect of the quadrant brings us the most happiness in different phases of life and gravitate towards it, as the most logical pursuit is happiness.

Anger

Anger can never yield fruitful results. Anger is a trap. Stay away from it.

There is perhaps only one problematic human emotion, and that is anger. The problem with anger is not that it exists within us, but how well we handle it. Anger is certainly not a sign of strength, especially when it is explosive. Undoubtedly, chronic angry outbursts, arguments, and flares of temper are detrimental to our health. They trigger the release of adrenaline, keeping us on high alert for a crisis. When this happens frequently, being in a constant state of high alert can lead to high blood pressure, clogged arteries, and an increased risk of stroke and heart attack. Our emotions are chemical, and these chemicals are released by the brain. We have the ability to control these chemicals. However, over time, these chemicals can alter our behavior and control us. After giving vent to our rage, we often regret many, if not all, of the things we said. Getting angry has never resolved problems. The more one gives in to anger, the more addicted they seem to become. Behaviors repeated over time rewire the brain, establishing neural networks. This means that anger breeds more anger. Anger also affects your body, causing cells to lose their capacity to absorb nutrients, inhibit growth and rejuvenation, and negatively impact health.

You will find that most of the time, you are angry at a person, not a behavior pattern or an issue. If an issue is the source of anger, you can learn to channel that anger into energy and use it constructively. If a behavior is the cause, you can learn to find humor in it. If you are angry with a person, you have made a decision to be angry with them. It has been observed that if you are getting angry with someone, you are, in a way, getting angry with yourself. Your own negativity makes you view others negatively. Meditation can help you control your anger and cool down.

There is a Chinese proverb that says, "If you are patient in one moment of anger, you will escape a hundred days of sorrow." If we sit with our anger mindfully, we respond rather than react. Exploring your anger can provide valuable insights, and learning from the incident can help you approach things differently in the future. Somewhere along this journey, you will realize that you played some role in the situation. By acknowledging your part, you can use that knowledge to create more peaceful relationships going forward. And lastly, forgive. Express your love and forgiveness now, while you can still enjoy the peace it will bring you.

Family

All of us have people in our lives whom we keep coming back to again and again, making it impossible to leave them behind as we move forward. These are the people who are most important to us, offering unconditional love and being essentially non-judgmental, or perhaps they love us despite any judgments they may hold. A strong family unit takes care of our basic need to belong and strengthens our capacity to be individuals in our own right, enabling us to make well-considered decisions.

Those who are most precious to us are the ones with whom we can be ourselves, dropping all masks and erasing all boundaries. These are the people we can trust blindly. They are patient listeners when we need to vent and offer honest opinions without complaining or showing impatience. You can count on their love and their complete acceptance of you. Acceptance is a great human need; we yearn to be accepted as we are. The need to belong to a group or community is so strong that it influences some of the most important decisions of our lives. Belonging helps us find value in our lives and equips us to deal with loneliness, pain, and rejection. It is within the family structure that a child learns how best to deal with the outside world. A person's strength in later life depends largely on the self-reliance, self-appreciation, and values instilled in them during their early years.

Within a family structure, we learn to communicate effectively, provide support, make time for each other, and build positive relationships. This is where the foundation for our future relationships and effective communication is laid. Here, we simply belong by being ourselves. We do not feel the need to adjust our value system or beliefs to gain acceptance. Family instills moral values and shapes our personalities and beliefs. You will notice that the kind and wise words of family members have helped make you a better human being.

Our family can consist of blood relatives or close friends. From promoting your inner growth to providing financial support, your family helps you achieve your goals. With your family by your side, you need not feel lonely as you venture into the world. This team of people supports you, desires the best for you, and is always there for you when needed.

Mind And Thoughts

The power of the mind is one of the strongest and most useful faculties you possess. This power resides in your thoughts. The multitude of thoughts coursing through your mind are responsible for everything that happens in your life. These dominant thoughts influence your behavior and attitude, ultimately controlling your actions. As you think, so is your life!

Thoughts act as a video that plays on the screen of your mind. The type of thoughts in this mental video determines the kind of life you lead and the experiences you undergo. If you wish to make changes in your life, you must change the content of this mental video, selecting the thoughts you prefer.

You can train and fortify this mental power. You can utilize it to effect changes in your life and even influence the minds of others. Just as you plant seeds, nurture them, and provide them with nourishment to grow into healthy and robust plants, thoughts, like seeds, naturally tend to flourish and manifest in your life when nurtured with attention, interest, and enthusiasm.

Your thoughts transition from your conscious mind to your subconscious, guiding your actions in accordance with these thoughts. Your thoughts also resonate with other minds, so those in a position to assist you may offer their help, sometimes without even understanding why. The power of your mind aligns with the universe, meaning your thoughts are synchronized with its manifestation.

When you repeatedly dwell on the same thought, it accumulates the power to help you turn it into reality. By actively and consciously managing your thoughts, you become the master of your mind. Altering your thoughts leads to a transformation in your feelings, eliminating the triggers for those feelings. These changes usher in a higher level of inner peace.

Since you are both the thinker and the observer of your thoughts, it is essential to pay close attention to them in order to identify "who" is controlling them. This knowledge will determine which technique you employ to manage them. It is crucial to be vigilant daily, observing your thoughts and catching yourself when undesirable ones arise.

There are two primary methods to control your thoughts

Technique A—Interrupt And Replace Them: This approach serves as a means to reprogram your subconscious mind. Over time, the replacement thoughts will become your default mental state.

Technique B: Eliminate Them Altogether: This technique involves the removal of undesirable thoughts from your mental landscape.

Visualization

How can you harness the power of your thoughts?

Visualize a perfect scene representing whatever you wish to accomplish, as though you are the director of a movie. Infuse this mental imagery with vivid details, color, sounds, scents, and life. Repeatedly engage in this process of visualization while maintaining faith and meticulous attention. Your subconscious mind will embrace these mental scenarios as genuine experiences. It cannot distinguish between real and imaginary encounters, regarding both as actual. Consequently, it will begin to reshape your reality to align with the images in your subconscious mind.

Situations and objects that you consciously visualize regularly will eventually manifest in your real life. This manifestation does not occur overnight but requires time, coupled with your ambition, sincerity, and dedicated focus.

This technique is a powerful means to transform negative habits and cultivate new, positive ones. Apply it to attract wealth and possessions, secure a promotion at work, establish a successful business, enhance health and relationships, alter circumstances, and virtually any other endeavor.

Pay meticulous attention to the thoughts you allow into your mind. Strive to dismiss negative thoughts and welcome only those that yield positive, joyful, and constructive outcomes.

Your thoughts and imagination are the driving forces behind whether you fail or succeed. Learn how to visualize and achieve your dreams and goals.

When you visualize your dreams, you achieve them.

Creative visualization and law of attraction techniques to enhance your life, discover love, attract wealth, and realize your dreams and aspirations.

Prayers

Prayer is heartfelt communication with God from deep within. When we approach God with profound humility, imploring, and yearning for our desires, it is termed a 'prayer.' A prayer embodies respect, love, supplication, and faith. It conveys the devotee's sense of helplessness and surrender as they offer their actions to God. In simple terms, talking to God can be called prayer. It is the act of opening one's heart to the Almighty, revealing everything within. Praying is not a challenging task; prayer is merely being oneself and conversing with God honestly and sincerely. Prayer possesses incredible power, and it's crucial to remember that the words spoken in prayer have the potential to work miracles. Do not underestimate the potency of prayer. When tempted by adversity, turn to prayer. Prayer provides the strength to overcome, the fortitude to endure, and the faith to complete the journey set before us in this life. Let us not relegate prayer to a mere routine or habit but instead regard it as a spontaneous love poem, an expression of ourselves to God.

It has been observed that the more time we devote to the remembrance of God, the more our countenance radiates with the divine, and our character begins to reflect the loving nature of God. Profound changes manifest in our habits and lifestyles. We are compelled to relinquish selfishness and extend sincere love to others. Prayer transforms us from within, and this transformation becomes evident in our outward demeanor.

Attitude

A person with a golden heart and a positive attitude is the most beautiful individual in the world. Quoting Abdul Kalam, 'One beautiful heart is better than a thousand beautiful faces; choose people with beautiful hearts.'

Your attitude shapes the world in which you reside. It serves as the foundation for both your triumphs and your setbacks, both past and future. It has the power to make or break you. Your attitude is the architect of your life. The remarkable aspect is that you hold the reins to control it.

Attitude encompasses your sentiments toward people and circumstances. Your actions spring from your attitude, evoking responses from others. It is your attitude toward others that enables the universe to determine how it will respond to you. A positive and joyful attitude begets positive and joyful outcomes. Conversely, if you project a negative attitude, you have already met failure before you even begin.

Negative attitudes result from perpetually harboring negative thoughts until they infiltrate your subconscious and become an integral part of your personality. Over time, these attitudes become habitual, often without your awareness. Once you possess a negative attitude, you inevitably anticipate failure and disaster, which, in turn, attracts them to you like a magnet.

This cycle becomes self-reinforcing. You expect the worst, and the worst materializes, solidifying your negative convictions. To cultivate a new attitude, you must exert significant effort to change your subconscious thinking. This entails scrutinizing every thought until positive thinking becomes second nature. You cannot merely extinguish negativity; you must replace negative thoughts in your mind with positive ones. Admittedly, negative situations are an undeniable reality. However, it is your attitude that determines whether a situation is positive or negative. It's time to recognize that you have control over your thoughts and emotions—no one else on Earth possesses this power unless you relinquish it. Take charge of your attitude and your state of mind, and you will seize control of your outcomes.

Passion

It is impossible to achieve wealth or any form of success in life without passion or a deep-seated enthusiasm for what you do, whether it's the simplest task or the most complex endeavor. There comes a point where work, commitment, and pleasure converge, and you reach a profound wellspring where passion resides, making the seemingly impossible attainable.

Consider this: If you had a million dollars in the bank, what kind of work would you engage in? Would you abandon your mundane job in favor of something truly exciting— something you've always yearned to do?

Now ask yourself: Why aren't you pursuing that passion right now? Is it due to peer pressure or a reluctance to leave your comfort zone? Are you afraid to rock the boat? However, you might already be half asleep in your current routine. A boat rocking might jolt you awake and bring you to your senses.

Do not wait for dire circumstances to awaken you from your mediocre life. Make a conscious decision to live and work passionately, rendering your life meaningful. You have resolved to live fully and passionately and reap the rich rewards at the end of the rainbow.

Passion for your desires fuels success. It acts as the driving force, bridging the gap between your ambitions and your 'why,' the core motivation behind pursuing your desires. Passion is the stake you put on the table to demonstrate your commitment to victory. Without this motivating elixir, surmounting obstacles that may arise along your path to success can be challenging. As Warren Buffet wisely asserts, "When you're genuinely passionate about life and what you're doing, you'll rise early, stay up late, and dance your way to work."

Fight Your Negativity

We often dwell within our minds, sometimes to the point of living inside them. Many of us squander precious time worrying about the future, replaying events from the past, and fixating on aspects of life that leave us dissatisfied. Past experiences and situations, while devoid of power, regain it when we clutch them with painstaking detail. Regrettably, these unwanted thoughts can hinder your ability to savor the present, divert your focus from your core activities, and drain your energy, ultimately leading to anxiety and depression. The good news is that with dedicated practice, one can replace negative thinking patterns with thoughts that genuinely assist. This can bring about a significant improvement in your day-to-day happiness.

Our minds, being powerful instruments, possess the uncanny ability to persuade us of things that aren't inherently true. These unfounded thoughts serve to reinforce negative thinking patterns. Once you become adept at recognizing them, you can also learn to challenge them. We often possess the peculiar capacity to assume the worst possible outcome, blame ourselves for anything that goes awry, and perceive everything in black and white, disregarding the shades of gray. Engaging in a mental exercise that challenges negative thoughts can yield clarity. Whenever you encounter a distorted thought, pause immediately and assess its accuracy. Consider how you would respond if a friend spoke of themselves in a similar manner—wouldn't you offer a counterpoint to their negative viewpoint? Applying the same logic to your thoughts, inquire whether you are anticipating the worst outcome or unjustly assigning blame for an outcome that didn't align with your expectations. When you challenge your mind, it often counters with alternative outcomes or explanations different from your initial assumptions.

Grant yourself a respite from negative thoughts. By setting aside a designated amount of time, perhaps five minutes, to engage with these thoughts, you can learn to disengage from them. After the allotted time, set the thought aside and proceed with your day.

Whether consciously or unconsciously, we all engage in self-judgment and comparisons with others or their lives. Letting go of judgment can lead to greater ease. To break free from judgmental thoughts, recognize your reaction, observe it, and then release it. Another helpful technique is to adopt a "positive judging" approach. When making judgments about a person, yourself, or a situation, instead of a negative assessment, seek to identify a positive aspect.

Research indicates that expressing gratitude significantly impacts your levels of positivity and happiness. Even during challenging times, you can usually find, however small, things to be grateful for. Acknowledging the positive aspects of your life will naturally keep you connected to them. Maintaining a gratitude journal daily is a simple and effective way to achieve this.

Steer clear of family and friends who habitually complain. Their constant negativity can bring you down. You needn't dwell on their complaints or engage further. Redirect the conversation to a more positive topic or politely disengage. Protect your sunny outlook because you must realize that you can't change others; you can only change yourself. Ensure you also have positive individuals in your life who uplift and bring smiles to your face.

Different news outlets can be a source of distress. However, there's a distinction between being informed and being inundated with news. Having a news channel perpetually on in the background or receiving continuous news alerts on your smartphone bombarding you with gloomy updates throughout the day can be overwhelming. Scouring the web for news sometimes plunges you into a vortex of negativity. I'm not suggesting a complete avoidance of media, but rather moderation in consumption.

Of course, there are times when being upset or angry is perfectly justified, and putting on a happy facade during serious situations is not a sustainable approach. The key is not to dwell in negativity but to ultimately address and manage your emotions.

"A negative mind will never foster a positive life."

Every Great Story Happened When Someone Decided Not To Give Up

Spryte Loriano rightly said, "Every great story on the planet happened when someone decided not to give up but kept going no matter what."

Every great story begins with pain and failure. Today may be difficult to live, and tomorrow may be even worse, but the day after tomorrow will bring bright daylight. We may face rejection that acts as discouragement. Despite these setbacks, you can achieve greatness if you believe in yourself and possess the courage, determination, dedication, and competitive drive. If you are willing to sacrifice small pleasures in life for greater rewards, it can be done.

In a journey towards success, there will be numerous peaks and valleys, along with long stretches of smooth sailing that illuminate the path ahead. Any dirt clinging to your shoes will gradually fall away as you continue.

When problems arise, it's easy to consider quitting. However, these challenges should serve as motivation to persist. Your determination to never give up, no matter the obstacles, brings you one step closer to realizing your dreams. So, never let yourself give in; keep holding on and keep moving forward.

Three Important Rules To Remember

1. If you don't go after what you want, you'll never have it.

2. If you don't ask, the answer will certainly be no.

3. If you don't step forward, you'll remain in the same place.

Inspirational Stories

How often do you come across a stand-up comic who also works as a house helper? In India, extraordinary stories are not in short supply, and the tale of Mumbai resident Deepika Mhatre is no exception.

From selling imitation jewelry to passengers on local trains to working as a domestic helper in five households, life was a constant struggle for this 43-year-old. However, she chose to confront her challenges with humor. Her life took a turn when one of her employers hosted a talent show for house helpers a year ago. This event transformed Deepika's life. She was a resounding success in the talent show, which ignited her belief that she could pursue comedy full-time. Real life may lack fairy tales and godmothers, but things progressed gradually for Deepika. One opportunity led to another, and she eventually began performing comic sketches professionally. Her sketches draw from her own experiences as a house helper, shedding light on both the positive and negative aspects of her life.

"In my journey to becoming a comic, life became difficult, but I kept smiling. Now, I tell people to keep smiling and laughing. Never be afraid to dream, and make sure you have the dedication to work hard toward achieving those dreams. Through my performances, I want to convey that your domestic help is also human, and they deserve dignity."

This man's extraordinary life inspired the filmmakers of '3 Idiots' to create the unforgettable character of Phunsukh Wangdu. The 52-year-old engineer from Leh gained national attention when he founded a revolutionary school in 1988, admitting children marginalized by society as failures. Wangchuk's sole aim was to make learning enjoyable and practical, rather than subjecting children to rote memorization. Later, his groundbreaking innovations like 'Ice Stupas' and solar-heated mud huts brought him international recognition for finding sustainable solutions in challenging environments.

"More than inspiration, it was empathy that led me to find solutions to issues affecting common people. Whether it's the water problem or education for children, these are issues faced by people in need, and my deep empathy compelled me to address their problems. Empathy is a virtue instilled in me by my mother and ancestors. It's what makes us human, and it should come naturally. If we want India to be a great nation, we must strive to be great citizens first. We can begin by doing good for society."

The second-highest-paid actor in Asia, Rajnikanth, whose life story had a humble beginning, is now the biggest superstar ever. His film releases are celebrated like festivals by his fans, and his stardom knows no bounds. However, his journey was filled with challenges. Rajnikant hails from a lower-middle-class family in Bangalore, and he spent his early life in poverty. At the age of six, he started his education and was a bright student, but he was also mischievous, with a keen interest in sports and acting.

After completing his schooling, Rajnikanth took on various odd jobs, including carpentry and bus conductor, before pursuing his passion for acting. His family did not support him, but he received emotional and financial support from colleagues and friends. During his struggling phase, Rajnikanth was noticed, and from that point onward, he never looked back. His passion, dreams, hard work, and unwavering determination made him the second-highest-paid actor in Asia.

Quote by Rajnikanth: "God gives a lot of things to bad people, but He will let them fail eventually. God tests good people a lot, but He will never let them down."

Struggles, difficulties, and failures are part of everyone's life. No one can claim to have lived a life without challenges or failures. It's a misconception that successful people achieve wealth and success solely due to luck and never face failure. This is not true! Every individual in the world encounters problems and failures. The key difference between successful people and others is that successful individuals refuse to give up until they achieve their dreams.

People become successful when they possess the strength and courage to stand up after falling and continue pursuing their goals with the same determination they had in their minds.

As the saying goes, "Falling down is an accident, but staying down is a choice!" Successful people never stay down; they persevere in their pursuit of dreams and goals.

You Are A Masterpiece!

You are wonderfully made, a marvelous work of God. Do you believe that, or are you saying, "I wish I were taller? I wish I were slimmer. I wish I had a smaller nose, and then I will find success"?

My friend, it is best not to base your self-worth and ability to succeed on your looks or people's negative comments. Don't compare yourself with others, like the models in fashion magazines and other public figures who seem to have it all because of their looks. Without advocating for shabbiness, regardless of your height, weight, or nose size, you are what Nature made you—a masterpiece, a piece of art. Begin to see your true self and worth in the mirror, and be grateful for them daily. This will lead you to treat your body well and give you such inner beauty and strength that people can't help but want to treat you favorably!

You are an artist. Yes, you are, and your life is your art. Art is not just something in a museum; it's your life. I believe there's much more to life than eating, sleeping, and seeking pleasure. There must be something more beautiful and profound; otherwise, why were we not born as animals but as humans with a mind to think and remember?

Musicians play with instruments. Artists create with tools. But the true "artists" of life, like you and me, create with their hearts. It doesn't matter if you're a musician, a waiter, a parent, a teacher, or a mechanic. It doesn't matter if you're pouring coffee, scrubbing floors, trading shares, or coaching kids. You can be walking, sitting, speaking, or meditating. It's not "what" you do, but "how" and "where" you do it from. Are you connected with the rhythm of nature? Is your heart in tune with the universe? Every moment, you can create magic. At any moment, you can do something different from what you have been doing all this time. I urge you to let go of what you know. Let go of someone else's road map. Blaze your trail. Just because what you want to do has never been done before does not mean it cannot be done. That should be all the more reason to try it out, and never mind if you fail. At least you tried; you would have failed had you not tried at all. Dare failure! Defy the usual! It is best when you transcend what people tell you is impossible, especially those who have never done what you are seeking to do. You have something magical deep within your heart that wants to be given birth through you. It is the life force itself seeking to express itself through you.

By doing this, you will find out what happens. Your heart is your paintbrush, and the entire universe is your canvas. Your life is your art. Dare to make it a masterpiece? The most important masterpiece you'll ever create is your life. But to create your masterpiece, you must first design it. That is, you must have a vision of what it looks like. Once you have a vision and design it, you can begin the process of building it.

Asking a few questions to oneself can be the guiding light to a transformed life, such as:

- What matters most?

- What priorities drive you each day?

- What are you doing that makes you come alive?

- When you look back on your life, what do you want to be able to say about it?

- How do you want to feel?

- What have you wanted to accomplish?

- What legacy will you have left?

For some, the answers to these questions may lead them to a new career. However, for most, it will simply lead to changes that will align your life with the vision and design you have for it. You might realize that you are not spending enough time on your priorities, and therefore, your masterpiece is not developing as it should. Whatever your masterpiece looks like, your design will help you see what you need to do or stop doing to create it.

I also want to caution you to make sure you are building your masterpiece and not someone else's idea of what your masterpiece should be. You don't need to fulfill others' desires for you. Do what is the strongest desire in you that would lead to a vibrant life. Stand up to that strong feeling that there is something else for you. When you stop trying to create someone else's masterpiece and instead focus on designing and creating the masterpiece you are meant to build, you dedicate yourself to it and give it your all. You have one masterpiece to create, so design and build your masterpiece, not someone else's.

You must stay positive as you move from the design phase to the building phase. You could face challenges during the building process, but always remember, negative thoughts are the nails that build a prison of failure, but positive thoughts will build you a masterpiece.

It is best to stay flexible and adaptable throughout the process. Your plans could change, especially when they must give way to the ultimate creator's master plan. And lastly, you have to choose the right habits because what you do each day will become who you are. Your habits will transform your design, vision, and plans into the masterpiece of your life.

You have only one life, and you are the only artist to make your life work and turn it into a masterpiece. Therefore, this idea should remind you constantly that your life is your responsibility, and thus, give it all you've got. The greatest adventure of our lives is discovering who we are and spending time doing what brings out the best in us.

Embrace experimentation, as this world has come this far because a few people dared to dream and try. We thrive on change but hate changes, but the only way forward is change. You can't create anything worthwhile if you are not willing to experiment. Find inspiration from the greats and start exploring all possibilities.

The only way to succeed is to try. Nobody gets it right the first time. Artists experiment with different ideas until they find what works for them. Try and make mistakes. The painter Willem de Kooning used to wrap his paintings in newspapers between sessions, which kept the paint from drying out. This had the inadvertent effect of transferring some of the print into the painting. He liked the effect, so he utilized it and produced great effects in subsequent paintings.

"I experience a period of frightening clarity in those moments when nature is so beautiful. I am no longer sure of myself, and the paintings appear as in a dream." Vincent Van Gogh

Begin with the end in mind. Artists start with a clear idea of what they want to create—a brilliant image shining in their minds. Clarity of purpose keeps creativity on track.

"Life is a series of natural and spontaneous changes. Don't resist them; that only creates sorrow. Let reality be reality." Lao Tzu

Everything meaningful in life takes time and perseverance. One of the greatest impediments to living a fulfilling life is our impatience, the almost inevitable desire to hurry up the process, express something, and make a quick splash. Artists don't work like that. If you want to be the best at anything, you need to value the process. When you practice something—anything—you improve, you grow, you advance, and you gain a skill and heaps of confidence in the process because you get better with time. Focus on developing your craft.

"Don't limit your challenges; challenge your limits." Jerry Dunn

Challenge The Challenge

Life is replete with challenges. Some people seem to meet challenges in their lives with confidence, while others struggle to overcome them with relative ease. You gain a sense of satisfaction from facing challenges head-on, as it brings a sense of accomplishment and can be very fulfilling. On some level, you seek challenges. Your highest self wants you to learn and grow, and life's most effective tool toward growth is the experience of the challenge.

The crux of the problem is that very often you might find yourself facing the same challenges repeatedly, resulting in a loss of motivation to confront the issue and learn the lesson it has to convey. At that point, challenges can escalate into problems, spiraling into despair and frustration.

You can overcome these challenges with a sense of responsibility and awareness, where challenges are considered opportunities. Facing the challenge is the most important and obvious step, yet it is also the step most often missed. Instead of facing the challenge head-on, people spend time looking for a way around the issue or wallowing in despair at the enormity of the challenge. Putting a challenge off doesn't make it go away; the most important thing you can do is face it.

What can help you cope with facing the challenge is to be present now. We often underestimate the power of being present. If you make a practice of facing your challenges—even in failure—with complete presence and awareness, you will find that most challenges are not challenges at all.

Meditation can help you cope with it and is a good method to help you focus during difficult times. Questioning yourself can help you better understand the problem and how it affects you.

Ask yourself questions like, Why is this issue a challenge? Do I believe in my capability to successfully resolve this challenge? What are the possible outcomes if I succeed or fail?

These questions will not solve the problem; rather, they are meant to help bring you into a fuller awareness of the challenge and your emotional reaction to it.

Only you can solve the problem. Others can help you arrive at a clear understanding, but no one ever solves your problems for you. Even in circumstances where someone else is in authority, only you can decide for yourself how you will process the situation. The longer you spend looking for guidance outside of yourself, the longer you spend ignoring the problem. You can immediately stop looking for the easy way out. Make a decision by assessing the situation, your resources, and your abilities, and then act. You could seek others' help, but essentially, it will be your challenge to solve. Try facing the challenge at the earliest possible time; it will stop being a problem that much sooner.

There is a reason why certain challenges seem difficult to you while others breeze right through the same situations. There's a reason why you keep putting off a task for days, but others instantly do it. It's not because they are better than you or have a particular skill set or know-how that you don't. It's all about consciousness. They have found a way to avoid seeing those activities as challenges.

Challenges are, in essence, opportunities to grow. That growth takes place out of your potentiality, which is limitless and actively participating in every moment of your life. You are pure potential experiencing life through limitations, and challenges are spikes in that imaginary limitation barrier guiding you to awareness. With your potential, you can turn a mountain of challenges into a speck of dust.

Stressing about the outcome often turns a molehill into a mountain. Once your focus shifts to the activity you are doing, instead of the probable result, the most intimidating parts of the trial start disappearing. The moment you attach emotions to the problem, it gains an upper hand and has power over you. If you simply perform the task at hand without worrying about the outcome, you hold power over the situation. Remaining centered and fully aware, no challenge is too big to be overcome with power and grace.

Carelessness

Carelessness in life occurs when you lack the motivation to give enough attention and thought while taking actions in life, and it can play spoilsport. A little carelessness on your part may make the whole difference between success and failure in your life. It is a careless attitude that can destroy the chance of making your life full of interesting experiences, despite having all the requisite skills and expertise at your disposal. You tend to be careless when not focused or overconfident. For instance, while taking the flight back home from Dubai, my colleague and I were careless regarding the flight time. 'pm' was misunderstood as 'am,' and we missed our flight. We had to purchase new tickets, which proved to be very expensive. If we are not paying adequate attention to the activity we are involved in, it can take a toll on our lives.

Carelessness occurs when the mind becomes entangled with thoughts from the past or the future rather than paying full attention to the task at the present moment. As the mind drifts away, you have to train it to stay focused at the present moment to avoid being careless. Cluttering your mind with anger, worry, frustration, and grudges from the past does not play any significant role in the present moment but keeps you from paying full attention to the present situation. So it is better to declutter your mind and focus on the task of the present, however small or big, to avoid being careless in life.

Hurry invariably leads to carelessness. Doing things in a hurry to get things done without dedicating your full attention to what you are doing This can lead to chronic time pressure to complete tasks urgently. You would be better off practicing patience and waiting for things to fall into place. If you always remain in a hurry to get things done, you may make yourself vulnerable to carelessness, which, in turn, can make you experience tension, anxiety, frustration, guilt, etc. later on. So it is essential to avoid hurrying in life by doing things appropriately and with complete focus.

To make your life free from carelessness and enriching experiences, it is important to give importance to everything, whether big or small, and dedicate your full attention to them. Life always unfolds itself in the present moment. So learn to live in the present moment and do not let your mind drift away to the future or the past to avoid carelessness in life. Hence, life is too short to toss it here and there due to carelessness. You are born to make your life great by being careful. You have to remember that you only live once, and there are opportunities all around you waiting to get noticed, but you cannot make use of opportunities by being careless in life. Do not let your attitude of being careless set the tone of your life, for which you might regret it later. Make a conscious effort to be careful so that you can make your life worthwhile.

Truth And Honesty

Honesty takes you places in life that you never could have dreamed of, and it's the easiest thing you can practice to be happy, successful, and fulfilled. Cutting through deception, deceit, and lies, only honesty leads to a fulfilling, free life.

Honesty is about being real with yourself and others about who you are and what you want. Honesty equips us to become consistent, helps sharpen our perception, and allows us to have clarity of observance about everything around us.

The worst type of lying we could practice in order to deceive is when we lie to ourselves. We start messing around with our concept of morality, right and wrong, as well as our dreams and desires. When you look back on it, every time you lied, you were trying to excuse or misrepresent your shortcomings or to compensate for something, pursuing a sinful desire that would only, at best, produce temporary pleasure. The temptation of lying, ease of use, and false promises would get you nowhere in the end. You stay right in your tracks, or, much worse, go backward.

Honesty and seeking the truth are always the paths to take. Honesty engenders confidence and faith, empowers our willpower, and improves our vitality.

Telling the truth when tempted to lie can significantly improve a person's mental and physical health, according to a "Science of Honesty" study.

Respectable, admired behavior is always carried out with honesty. Telling the truth and supporting it with actions shows respect for what's right and develops esteem for ethical and moral integrity. Honesty is one of the key components of character and one of the most admired traits of a successful, responsible person.

Business transactions and the everyday transactions of human relations must be carried out with a code of trust and honesty, or else everything will break down. Honesty would endear you to many people of influence and, simply, to your friends and loved ones. Honesty is never contrived or inauthentic.

There's no coincidence that perhaps the most respected American in history, President Abraham Lincoln, was shrewd, direct, and honest in all of his human relations transactions and dealings. He was fair and just, a lesson he learned as a store clerk in dealing with customers at an early age. Lincoln's own words on the topic: "Resolve to be honest at all events; and if, in your judgment, you cannot be an honest lawyer, resolve to be honest without being a lawyer. Choose some other occupation."

Honesty cuts through red tape, distraction, frustration, and indecision. Honesty gets you where you want to go faster because you live how you feel, but your intuition will give you a feel for what is in harmony with your heart. Honest intentions in both speech and action earn the attention and respect of others. These people will invariably influence you. The company we keep and surround ourselves with helps define our outlook on life as well as lift us to places we couldn't have arrived at entirely by our efforts.

You have to start today by being as honest as you can with yourself. Be honest about your thoughts, words, actions, and wants. Then think about your interactions with society and your relationships. You can let people know your true self because you are not afraid of anything.

You Write. We Publish.

To publish your own book, contact us.

We publish poetry collections, short story collections, novellas and novels.

contact@thewriteorder.com

Instagram- thewriteorder

www.facebook.com/thewriteorder

www.ingramcontent.com/pod-product-compliance
Lightning Source LLC
LaVergne TN
LVHW041225080526
838199LV00083B/3395